My Story Thanh Nguyen

DEAR ROGER

Thank you for reading my book
I hope you enjoy it.

[signature]

To order additional copies, please contact us.
BookSurge, LLC
www.booksurge.com
1-866-308-6235
orders@booksurge.com

THANH
NGUYEN

MY STORY
THANH NGUYEN

2005

My Story Thanh Nguyen

To My Son Michael ...

*I have been waiting so long for this day—the day that you gradu-
ate from college. You are the first college graduate in my family, not
because no one wanted to go to college, but because no one could. We
lived in Vietnam, where there was no freedom for anything, let alone
to pursue education for a family like mine.*

*When my younger brother, Danh, was 12 years old, he went to
school to become a priest. He was a very smart boy and attended the
school for five years, until 1975. But then Saigon fell, the Communists won the war, religion was outlawed, and all the private schools
were closed. So Danh came back home and attended public school.*

*He finished high school and applied to college—he wanted to be a
pharmacist—but the Communists would not accept his application.
Our father had worked for the old government (and had been mur-
dered for it) and two of his sisters had fled Vietnam. So, Danh was
not permitted to go to college, nor did I ever have an opportunity to
do so. This is why I always wanted you to have an education and to
finish college. I wanted you to have what I couldn't have. I wanted
your life to be better than mine.*

*Now I want you to have something else: my story. This book is for
you. For a long time, I dreamed of writing this book. Finally, my
dream has come true, more than 30 years later.*

*Dreams are very important, and I want you to have your own and
for them all to come true. You mean so much to me, more than I can
ever tell you. When you were little, you made me laugh, and when
you were a teenager, you never made me sad. And now, you are a*

grown man and so understanding and eager to help me in the store, but I don't think you can do that anymore. You have your own dreams to pursue, and I want you to follow them. But I also want you to remember that life is not easy. Sometimes, dreams don't come true for many years, but if you are strong and hopeful and pray to God, you will be fine.

PREFACE

I was born in Vietnam on September 11, 1954, and reborn on that day in 1978. It was on that day that I left Vietnam—no—I escaped Vietnam—and went to Holland. Today, I live in Maryland (in the United States), with my husband and son. I have my own dry cleaning and tailoring business, a beautiful home, a nice car, and all the clothes and jewelry I could want. I am not rich, nor poor. I am an American, but 24 years ago, I had nothing but a small place on a crowded, leaking boat on the South China Sea. With the man who later became my husband, I was running away from war, and fear, and death, and making my way toward a new life.

Most of my family remained in Vietnam—10 of my 11 brothers and sisters, and, of course, my mother. And even now, so many years later, not a day goes by that I do not think of them and the troubles they continue to endure. That is why I work everyday, as I always have—to help them survive and live more comfortably in that hard country.

But every year on my birthday, I also reflect on my life in Vietnam during the war and recall what my family and I went through and what my mother and I endured. Those experiences stand out clearly and vividly in my mind, and I feel them in my heart. I have never told this story to anyone before, but now my son Michael is grown, and I want him to know.

CHAPTER 1
My Father

My story begins in 1966, when I was 12 years old. My father, Bo Van Nguyen, was the mayor of our village, Tan Loi, which was in the southern part of Vietnam. My father had been mayor for as long as I could remember, and he was well respected by the villagers. They called him "Mister Bo." Because of his position and the power that it gave him, he received many privileges, and our family lived well.

Ours was the largest and most beautiful house in our village— made of wood, very tall, and with many rooms. It stood at the end of a long driveway, lined all the way with flowers. Fruit trees grew in the yard—mango, papaya, and banana. Beyond this grew ten acres of rice fields and eight acres of coconut trees. I thought it was a paradise. Life was wonderful. We had plenty of food, a radio (the first in our village), and everyday we went to Catholic school. I lived like a princess, and I thought it would last forever. Being only 12, I thought little of the war, even though it was close by.

I was also unaware that my father's position was very dangerous. He was part of the "old government," and the Communists—who controlled the jungles nearby, and who had spies in Tan Loi—were watching him. From time to time, Communist soldiers would sneak into our village at night and take people away. They would have taken my father away if they could have, so he lived apart from our family, in the mayor's compound with his bodyguards and soldiers. There he was safe, but if he had ever come home, even for a short visit, the Communists would have had their chance to take him. Sometimes he would visit anyway, to see my mother and us children. This was always dangerous, but I guess he could not stay away.

My parents had 11 children, and my father took very good care of us. We always had enough to eat and enough money to go to school everyday. He was a good father, and I loved him. He was tall, handsome, and very sweet. A good man, but not perfect.

My father had many girlfriends and had three other children with two of these women. This was not uncommon for a Vietnamese man at that time, but it was still not right. My mother knew everything. It hurt her very much, but she never complained to my father, nor did she ask him to stop. In fact, at one point, my father had asked her if he could have a girlfriend, and my mother had agreed.

The reason my father wanted a girlfriend was because he really wanted a son. Vietnamese men desired a son perhaps more than anything else, and my parent's first six children had all been girls. My father loved his daughters, but he was disappointed by the birth of one girl after another. I guess at some point, he decided that my mother would never give him the son he desired, but possibly, another woman would, so he asked my mother to let him try. She loved my father very much, perhaps more than any other woman ever did, and she knew what he yearned for. I think she may have agreed with him—possibly recognizing that she might never produce a son of her own.

So my father made himself available and soon met a woman who eventually gave birth to his two sons. He also had a daughter with another woman. These women lived in Tan Loi, at opposite ends of the village bridge, and he would occasionally visit them.

My parents continued to have children, however. Their seventh was a boy—finally—but he did not bring my father all the way back to my mother. This baby soon became ill and died.

More children followed. Another boy, this time, the one who lived— my brother, Thang. Then another girl, then I was born, then one more girl, and finally, another boy. Eleven children were born, but only six girls and two boys lived.

By 1966, only four of us still lived with our mother in the family home. My sister Diep and her husband, my younger sister Cong, my younger brother Danh and I. Later that same year, my father retired from his position as mayor. He could no longer live in the mayor's compound, but he could not move back home with us, either. The Communists still wanted him. So when he retired, he went and lived with my grandmother (my mother's mother) in Cai Nhum, a village far away on the other side of the Mekong River.

The Tan Loi River, which took my mother and me into Communist territory.

But even there, he was not safe, at this time. There was a great deal of fighting and many arrests. So after a few months, my mother and father decided that it would be better for him to live in Saigon, a big city where he could blend in and hide. But before he moved to Saigon, he came back home to stay with us for just a few days. He thought that he would be safe.

Those days my father lived with us were wonderful. But on the third day, I remember hearing my parents talking. Mother was worried and told him that he should leave for Saigon as soon as possible. He was not safe in Tan Loi, she said.

My father agreed and decided to leave the next morning at 6 a.m. I remember that, later that day, my sister, Diep, ironed my father's clothes for the trip—black pants and a white shirt. Then she hung them on a peg by the front door.

But in the early hours of the morning, around 4 a.m., someone knocked on our door. My mother answered it and found three men, wearing shorts, no shirts, and carrying guns. Their voices woke me up, but my younger brother and sister (with whom I shared a room) remained sleeping. I lay in bed and listened.

"Is your husband home?" a man asked. His voice was mean, and I was now scared.

"Yes," my mother answered. "What do you want?"

"We need to talk to him."

She let the men in, they sat down at our table, and then my mother went to get my father.

I heard his footsteps coming down the hall, then I heard him go to the table and sit down. My mother remained standing.

"We need you to come with us," the man said to my father.

"Why?" mother asked, interrupting my father, sounding very scared.

"We need to teach him something," said the man. This was when my mother knew that something bad was going to happen.

"But he'll be back in three days," the man continued, trying to reassure her. "Just three days, and he'll be back."

But my mother knew better. "Let me go instead," she pleaded. "He is old, his eyes are bad, and he cannot see well at night. I'll learn whatever you want him to learn, and I will teach it to him."

"No," said the man. "You can't go. We need him. But don't worry. In three days, he'll be back."

My mother was afraid. Maybe she knew that he would never come back. The Communists had come like this for other people in our village, people we had known, and no one with any power or importance like my father had ever been seen again.

My mother was now frantic. I could hear it in her voice.

"Please, let me go," she begged. "Let him stay. He's old. He's sick." By now, she was crying.

"No," he replied. My mother continued to beg him, but he was adamant. This happened many times.

All during this conversation, my father had said nothing, but now he tried to reassure my mother.

"Don't worry," he said. "I'll be back. It's just three days. Don't worry." But he was scared, too, and his words were not reassuring.

At some point, I had gotten out of bed and left my room, and by this time, I was standing next to my mother. I had seen and heard everything.

Father was still dressed for bed, and I remember him standing up and walking to the front door. He took his pants and shirt down from where my sister had hung them and put them on. Then he said something quietly to my mother and walked out with the three men.

My mother went after him.

"Can I come with you?" I asked.

"No," she said. "Stay here. Wake up the others."

I wanted to go with her, but I never disobeyed my mother. She left and I ran into my bedroom and woke my brother and sister. I told them what had happened, and we sat together, so scared and worried.

I was so upset. I could not sit still. I tried to stay in the house like I had been told, but I soon left my brother and sister and ran after my parents.

I caught up with them, but no one seemed to notice me. My mother was crying and pleading with the men. The one man who had done all the talking, the leader, was still telling her that she should not worry, that my father would be back in three days. But the other men were close to my father, watching him carefully, preventing him from escaping. He was silent. I thought then that I would never see him again.

We soon came to the river that ran near our house, the Tan Loi. The river is not wide—maybe 25 feet across—and the water was very low at that point, so we walked across in the mud. I walked next to my mother and she next to my father. My father was surrounded by the three men.

One of my older sisters, Hanh, lived on the other side of the river, and when we arrived near her house, she was outside waiting for us. When we came near, she cried and begged the men, who did not stop. So she joined us and followed, too. We all wanted to see where they were taking father. But at the edge of the village, the men stopped us. We were not allowed to go any farther.

The men walked on with my father. We cried out for him, screamed our good-byes, then waited until he was no longer in sight. This was the last time any of us ever saw him.

No one slept any more that night. Our family gathered at my house—five of my nine brothers and sisters. We sat up all night in the living room and talked and cried. No one believed what the man had said, that our father would be back in three days. We knew better, we knew about the Communists, and we knew that when people like my father were taken away, they didn't come back, or if they did, they were not the same.

CHAPTER 2
Into the Jungle

Another fear soon gripped us: What would happen to us? The Communists could come back and take us away. This happened. Sometimes they took entire families away. We needed to leave our home and village, but at the same time, we couldn't. Not yet. What if our father did come back? It was possible, and we had to be here if he did.

So we waited, praying that he would return, and that the Communists would not.

On the third day, father did not return, as the man had promised. But a friend of my father's did arrive, and he had news. He had seen my father, who had asked that we send him money, cigarettes, and a blanket. We gathered what he needed and gave it to his friend.

For the next few days, we continued to wait, because we now knew that he was still alive. After about a week, our father's friend returned and told my mother that she could see our father, if she brought money. He said it would be very dangerous, because she would have to go into Communist territory, into the jungle. There would be a path she could follow, but there would be mines, and traps, and soldiers. My mother decided to go anyway. She had to see our father, and she could not wait any longer.

She left a few days later, and I went with her, just like I always did when she had to do something frightening. She took me because she said I was so fast and so brave. Nothing seemed to scare me. Of course, that was not true. I was just 12 years old and many things scared me. Bombs, the Communists, the jungle. But I could always think and make my body do whatever needed to be done, even when I was afraid.

We left very early in the morning, in the dark. No one else in the village could be allowed to see us, and no one could know where we were going, because they would think that we were collaborating with the Communists, and that would make trouble. We made our way quietly through the village to where one of my sisters kept a small wooden boat along the riverbank. The boat was flat and low, and I was afraid. But we soon freed it from the shore, and my mother used a long bamboo pole to push us out away from Tan Loi.

After a while, we pulled up at a place on the riverbank, not far from where the Tan Loi meets the Mekong River. Somehow, my mother knew that this was where we were to stop and get out. We tied the boat to a tree and began to walk away from the river, toward the jungle.

We soon crossed a small bamboo bridge. On the other side of it, the jungle began. We stopped. I was very scared. The sun had not fully risen, and it was still dark. The trees and plants in front of us were thick, so we could not see too far. It was also hot, humid, closed in, and very quiet.

But we walked in and kept walking for many hours, following the path, praying all the time for God to protect us from mines, tigers, and guns. Finally, we came out of the jungle into an open area of rice fields. A small wooden hut stood in a clearing. My mother and I stopped and stared at it from the edge of the jungle. It was not really a hut, it was more like a large box, and we knew that father was inside of it. By now, it was late morning, and the sun beat down on the hut. It had no windows, just a door, and the door was closed. It must have been more than 100 degrees inside.

A man approached us. We gave him the money he wanted and waited to be taken to father. But then, he told us that we were not allowed to see him. My mother cried out.

"Why? Why can't we see him?"

"No," said the man. "You cannot see him."

"I'll do everything you want," she begged. "Why?" She didn't understand. She had been told that we would see father, and she had believed it. Why wouldn't the man listen? What had changed?

"Listen," said the man. "Be quiet, and do not ask questions."

We stood quietly for a moment, and then we understood. We had been tricked. We were now in Communist territory, and since my father was a leader in the old government, this man thought that we had a lot of money and would give them more. That's all he wanted. Money.

Just then, an airplane flew high overhead. A jet, probably an American military jet. The man became very angry, and we could see that he was scared.

"Did you bring this plane?" he screamed. "Are you trying to trick us?"

We had not, and we tried to make him believe us. But he did not.

"If we are bombed, if you have tricked us, you will die. We will shoot you."

We had not brought the plane, we had not tricked anyone, but the plane could drop its bombs anywhere, even here. My mother and I prayed to God. The man was tense and very angry. We prayed and begged him as the plane flew overhead. It did no good.

"I'll shoot you both," he screamed.

But eventually, the plane passed on, and the man slowly relaxed. I don't remember what happened next, but we soon left, having not seen father, and not even knowing if he were still alive. We walked back to the river—three or four hours more of walking and crying, a journey back void of the hope we had started with.

CHAPTER 3
Murder and Escape

During this trip through the jungle, both my mother and I got poison ivy very badly and became very sick—infections and high temperatures. We needed a doctor, but if my mother had called for one, she would have had to explain how we got it, and that would have led to trouble. So we cared for ourselves as best we could and were very sick for about two weeks. Eventually, it got so bad that our family thought we might die, so someone sent word to a friend of my father's—Bac Tu—a very old man, who healed people with plants.

Bac Tu came to our house, carrying leaves of special plants that he grew on his property. He sat by our beds and prepared his medicine. He crushed the plants, mashed them into a paste, and placed it on our wounds. It felt comforting and cooled down right away. After a few days of this treatment, we were well again and returned to our search for my father.

But a few days later, my older sister, Diep, walked outside of our house and found a large paper sign hung on a tree in the yard. Someone had put it there during the night. Walking closer, she realized that it was from the Communists. It said our father was dead, that he had been killed because he was a "criminal," and the sign listed the "crimes" of which he had been found guilty. There were about 20 of them, and they were all lies. He had done nothing. The Communists had killed my father because he was powerful and respected and part of the old government, and they hated him for that.

My sister pulled the sign off the tree and ran inside. We all read it, then cried and cried.

"Why, God?" my mother cried out again and again, her arms above her, her head tossed back, her eyes searching heaven for some kind of answer. But no answer ever came, and we were left with the harsh truth that the Communists could do whatever they wanted. There were no rules for them.

I will never forget that moment. I can still see my mother and hear her grieving.

After a while, who knows how long, my mother put the sign away, and we never saw it again. I think she eventually burned it, many years later. She would also never remarry. My father had been her love.

A few weeks later, very early one Saturday morning, I was at the market, buying food, and I overheard some adults talking. They said that the Communists had arrested a friend of my father's, a man named Ba Nhi. He was being tortured and questioned because the Communists thought they would learn important information about the old government. I went home to tell my mother, but she already knew about Ba Nhi. News had a way of getting around quickly among the adults in our village.

Ba Nhi knew nothing about anything important, but the Communists did not believe him and a few days later, they killed him. I saw his body. The Communists had dumped it in the road. His hands had been tied behind his back with wire, and his throat had been cut. His head hung at an odd angle, and I could see the muscles and tendons in his neck. His wife and children were there, and other people from our village. Again, there was so much crying and wailing.

And fear, too. The murder of Ba Nhi was a warning to us all. My mother knew the Communists; she knew what kind of people they were. They could kill us all, and so she decided that we would have to leave— my mother and me and my younger brother and sister. I remember when she told us.

"We can't live here anymore," she said. "The Communists will come back and kill me."

Normally, my mother would not have told us anything. Vietnamese parents never explain anything to their children. One day they would just leave their home and their children would simply go quietly with them. But this situation was more serious and dangerous than anything that had ever happened before, so she talked to us, perhaps to help us feel less afraid.

My older sisters, Diep and Hanh, would stay in Tan Loi. Even though they were the daughters of Mister Bo, the "criminal," they would be safe because their husbands were from other families and, therefore, not involved. That is how Vietnamese society worked. The husband was everything, and that is why my mother had to leave.

Diep packed our things—just a few clothes for each child. My mother chose a wooden table and a bed that was large enough to hold all four of us. We gathered some wood and dry grass so we could cook our food and carried an old lighter. We also filled a tall, clay urn with water from our well. And that was all. We left everything else. But I felt even worse because I was just 12 years old. I left our happy and privileged life behind me, as well.

CHAPTER 4
Kien Hoa I

My mother had arranged for a local man to take us away in his boat. Other than this man, few people outside our family knew of our plans. We had to be careful, so we told just a few friends who, we knew, could keep a secret. They felt bad for us, but understood why we were leaving.

One morning, the man came and tied his boat up along the bank of the river near our house. I remember the boat. It was wooden, 10- by 25-feet, with a motor and a small roof in the middle. The man waited for us while we carried our things down the driveway to the riverbank. My brother-in-law and sister helped, but we still went back and forth many times. At the river, the man helped us load the table and bed. After everything was in place, my mother, younger brother, sister, and I got on and found a small, open place to sit. It was very tight and uncomfortable.

When everything was ready, the man started his motor, and we headed downstream, waving goodbye to our family, who stood on the riverbank.

We traveled for about half an hour, until we reached the Mekong River, which is much larger than the Tan Loi. This part of the Mekong was safe—no Communists, no fighting. We traveled out in the middle of the river. I remember seeing plants that drifted with the current, just below the surface of the water. I had nothing else to do, no one wanted to talk with, so I watched these plants float by for hours.

After four or five hours, we arrived at the city of Kien Hoa, where my family had friends who would let us stay with them. They lived in a simple house near a canal, and I remember that our living quarters were very small—just one room, with the kitchen, dining area, and beds, all together. This was a normal house for most Vietnamese people, and was better than the house of a poor person, but it was so different for us. Just a few hours earlier, we had lived in our big, beautiful house in our own village, and now we lived in a strange village with few belongings, in a single room. Oh, how our lives had changed. I remember how we cried. It was really strange for me, being in this new place, with new people. I was very sad and saw nothing but darkness in front of me. I had no idea what was to come, what would happen next, or how long we would stay. I only saw a black future.

We lived there for just a few nights and then moved to another house in the same neighborhood, but it was even worse. It, too, was very small, but this was the house of a poor person, with a thatched roof and walls. There was no room for our bed, so we slept on the bamboo bed that was already there. It had no mattress, just a thin cloth, and was very uncomfortable. I did not sleep very well. We stayed here for a little more than a month, and even though it was small and uncomfortable, we prayed every night that we could remain, because we had nowhere else to go.

We never felt safe. We always feared that the Communists would come for us. Plus, my mother was a very pretty woman, and since she was without a husband, men were always making advances towards her. But she didn't want anybody. I remember one man who would hang around our house at night. He was often drunk. He scared my mother, and she tried to drive him away, but he would always return drunk and say unpleasant things.

One day, my mother met a man who worked for the city government. He had a motorcycle, and his job was to ride through the streets, talking to people and trying to help them with their problems. My mother and the man began to talk, and it turned out that he was a relative. His name was Ton Nguyen, a cousin of my grandfather. Right away, he invited my mother and all of us to come live with him and his family in their house.

My mother refused; she was far too polite to accept such an offer, even from a relative. He was clearly a rich man, and we had no money at all. It would not have been proper. People would have thought that we were taking advantage of him, just because he was rich.

But the man persisted, my mother continued to refuse, and they bargained for some time—discussing other arrangements and other ways of paying.

Eventually, my mother accepted this offer: We would live on his property, but not in his house. Behind his house stood an old building where he had once kept chickens. He said it was big enough for all of us, and it was no longer in use and was now empty and clean. We would live there.

His home was just 10 minutes away from where we lived, so we went to take a look—our new-found relative went on his motorcycle, and the rest of us went in a hired rickshaw.

He lived in a huge house, an old, French mansion. He wasn't just rich. He was *very* rich. His house was surrounded by a high brick wall topped with broken glass. When we saw that, my mother and I both began to feel safer. If we lived here, it would be very hard for anyone to get in and take us away.

The man took us inside his house and showed us around. It was like a castle or a palace, and he insisted again that we live there with him and his family. But again, my mother refused. I knew what she was thinking. This house was too big, too fine, and too much like our old house. We had learned that sometimes such finery brings trouble, and we were tired of trouble. The chicken house would be fine, and indeed it was.

The building was long and quite large—about 15-feet wide and 25-feet long—and empty except for wooden posts down the center. The floor was cement, which was better than our old house in Tan Loi, which had a clay floor. And the roof was very fancy—terra cotta shingles the color of peaches. There was one door and one small window. The chickens had long gone, but their smell still lingered.

Ton Nguyen told us that whatever we needed, he would get for us, but I knew that my mother would never ask for anything. Already, this day had been like a dream. Having come to a strange city with nothing, we had now found a rich relative on whose property we were now living, behind his high, stone wall. We were safe, we were together, and we knew that we would find a way to survive. We were all very happy. We soon moved our things from the old place, and our bed and table and our love for each other made this chicken shack a home. That night, for the first time since leaving Tan Loi, we slept well.

CHAPTER 5
Soi and Keo

The first thing next morning, my mother made an oven out of rocks from the yard. She was a good baker and made tasty sticky rice sweets called soi and a kind of taffy called keo. Nearby was a market called Cho Lac Hong. Our plan was that she would cook and I would sell the soi at the market and the keo to candy vendors throughout the city. We had to make money to buy food, and this was the only way we knew how to do so.

Every morning at 4 a.m., mother would wake me up. I would help her cook a big pot of rice and prepare the *soi*. At first I was sleepy and not very helpful, but she would tell me what to do and I would do my best to accomplish it. After we had cooked the rice, and it had cooled, we'd place some on a banana leaf, sprinkle sugar and coconut on top, and roll it up. We placed them in a big, flat basket, and when it was full—and quite heavy—I would lift it in my arms and set off for the market. I also carried a few coins tightly grasped in one hand so I could make change, if I sold any.

The market was about 15 minutes away and walking was not easy. Sometimes I would have to hurry, because I had to reach the market by 6 a.m. We had rented a small spot of earth, and I had to be there on time or else my customers would go elsewhere for their *soi*. But I don't think I was ever late. I spent the morning at the market. I was shy and felt very insignificant and alone, but there was no one else to do it. My mother had to stay with my brother and sister, who were too young to be left alone.

The market was a large open area of dirt and cement. There were no trees, and in the summer, it was very hot. I always wore a big straw hat, black pants, a cotton blouse, and sandals.

I sold our sweets for 50 cents, which is equivalent to a few pennies today. It was very cheap. By 9 a.m., I usually sold all of the *soi*. But when I had some left over, I would have to find some way to sell them, because *soi* goes bad very quickly, especially in the summer. So I would call out to the people walking by and offer them a special price—two for the price of one. Since I was so young, I was naturally very quiet around the customers. Calling out to them and bargaining was difficult. I never got used to it, and I never liked it. Sometimes I would trade with other vendors who sold vegetables, sugar, meat, or fish. But sweets were so cheap that I would never get much in return. For example, I could trade six *sois* for one pound of vegetables, two fish, or for a piece of meat so small that it would fit in the palm of my hand.

Every once in a while I would get lucky and walk out our door and find a group of soldiers in the street. They would be on their way to the war and were always hungry. I would sit down on the curb across the street from them. Eventually they would walk over and buy everything I had. *Soi* was good for the soldiers. It is cheap and very filling.

When all the *soi* was gone, I'd take the money and buy ingredients for the next day, and then go back home to help my mother make *keo*.

I don't know where she learned the recipe, but we were all glad she had, because our *keo* was very popular and profitable. We would mix sugar, coconut milk, vinegar, and lemon juice in a pot, then cook it for a long time at a very low temperature. I had to sit beside the pot and stir without stopping so it wouldn't burn. If it burned, we would lose all the money we had spent on ingredients and have nothing to sell. So I would stir and stir until the candy turned yellow, and then I'd call my mother over so she could check it.

When it looked right, she'd draw a bowl of water from the well. Then using a stick, she'd drip a little candy into the water, where it cooled. She'd feel it with her fingers, checking for the right consistency.

When it was ready, she'd spread some cooking oil on the table and pour the candy in the middle so it could cool. Around this, she'd place more sugar that she'd mix with the candy. Nearby, a nail stuck out from one of the wooden posts. Mother would take the candy and hang it off the nail, and then pull it like a rubber band—wrapping it and pulling it, again, and again. I had never seen her work so hard.

When it was still a little soft, she'd put it back on the table, stretch it out once more, then cut it into small pieces. When these were cool and dry, we'd put the pieces in plastic bags and tie them with rubber bands. We supplied three local candy stands with our delicacy. The candy was very good. We were the only ones who made it, so it was in much demand.

After all the candy had been sold, I'd come home and gather wood for the fire, as well as fresh banana leaves for the next day's *soi*. I'd cut the leaves off the trees in the yard and lay them in the sun for 10 minutes or so, which would make them soft. Then I brought them inside and cut them into pieces, some large, others small. I cleaned them and prepared them for the next morning.

Everyday mother and I made between 100—200 pieces of *soi*, and each piece was made of three pieces of banana leaf, so preparation of the leaves took a lot of time. By 7 p.m., we would be finished with our work for the day. Although I was just 12 years old, I'd work like this everyday—13 hours a day. But I did not complain, nor was I angry or disappointed. The normal concerns of children—toys, games, clothes, movies, and friends—never entered my head. There was no time to play with others. I knew just one thing: My family needed me to work, and that's what I did, day after day, for the next three years.

CHAPTER 6
Kien Hoa II

Life was now better—we had a safe house and some money—but we were still so scared of what could happen. We also never looked back; it was too painful. We just worked, made money, and survived. My mother would never complain or talk about how she felt, but sometimes I would hear her crying in the night. During the day, she would never smile. She had lost her smile. We both had. I grew up very fast, and she grew very old.

For a while, however, there was one bright spot: school. The wife of our relative, Lai, was a teacher. A few months after we arrived in Kien Hoa, she arranged for me and my brother and sister to attend school in Phu Khuong, a small town a few miles away.

Since I was always so busy in the mornings, we mainly went to school in the afternoons. The three of us would walk, but the walk was often terrible and frightening.

From time to time, there would be fighting in the night between the Communists and the government soldiers. Occasionally on our way to school, we would pass by corpses and severed body parts on the road. Sometimes, the bodies would not be taken away for a week or more, so everyday we would see how they would turn green, and then blue over time in the heat. The smell was horrible. Flies swarmed over the bodies.

Eventually, the fighting reached our school. The Communists attacked it with artillery shells, destroying it completely. No one was hurt, because it happened at night, but our school had to be rebuilt. This happened more than once, but each time, the school was rebuilt.

This fighting could have reached us in Kien Hoa at any time. During this period, we rarely got a good night's sleep. We never knew if we would be attacked, or if we would be taken away. My mother began to save as much money as she could, just in case we ever had to leave again in a hurry. At the end of each day, no matter how little money we had, she would place a small amount of it in a can that stood in one corner of our house.

This went on for about a year—cooking and selling, cooking and selling—until one day, I felt a great pain in my left leg. I could no longer walk. This was very bad, because now, I could not go to the market. We would have no money and no food.

Mother hired a bicycle cart and took me to the hospital, to the section where poor people could get free treatment. There I was placed in a room with many other people, and then put in a bed with two others. I was in great pain. I couldn't move my leg, and I was afraid I would never walk again. My mother stayed with me—day and night. She slept on the floor and cared for me, and she did not complain. I felt guilty because while she stayed with me, no one was working and earning money for the family.

The doctors came and went, but since we had no money, they took no X-rays and gave me no medicine. They never discovered what was wrong with me. About a week later, a doctor told my mother that they could do nothing for me, and that we should go home, even though I was no better.

At home, I sat in bed while my mother prepared *soi* for my younger sister, Cong, to sell. Since she was just 11 years old, she could not go to the market, but would sit in front of our house and sell what she could.

A few days later, my mother was told of a doctor who might be able to help, but he would cost money, more money than we had. My mother decided to contact my older sister, Diep, who still lived in Tan Loi with her husband. Maybe she had some money, or could get some.

And so my mother sent her a message by bus. There were no telephones or telegraph services that we could use during this time. So my mother went to the bus station, found some people who were on their way to Tan Loi, and asked if they would find Diep and tell her that I was sick and that we needed money for a doctor. The stranger that mother located agreed to help us. Vietnamese people can be very kind.

The next day, Diep arrived with money. She had borrowed it from a neighbor, a man she knew, and because they were neighbors, he had charged her no interest, gave her no payment deadline, and presented no contract for her to sign. She simply thanked him and promised to pay him back, and that was enough.

A few days later, my mother and Diep took me to this new doctor. Since I could not walk on my own, they supported me—one on each side—as we made our way through the city.

I remember the doctor well, a friendly man about 50. He was very busy, too. Many people were sick at this time, but he gave me his attention. I sat down, and he began to examine my leg. Taking out a little rubber hammer, he tapped my right knee. It leaped in response. Then he tapped my left knee, and while it did not move like the other, it did twitch. The doctor smiled and sighed, then leaned back happily.

"You will walk again," he declared.

We all smiled. This was such wonderful news.

He gave my mother some medicine, and told her that I needed to take it everyday, and walk as much as I could, as soon as I felt able.

I took the medicine, and a few days later, I felt well enough to walk a little. Then I began to push myself. I had to get better. My family needed me. So I worked very hard.

"You can do it," I would tell myself. "You have to."

I also prayed to God. "Please, God," I prayed, "make me well. I can't be like this."

Slowly, day by day, week by week, I began to improve. I could feel it. After about a month (a month in which we made no money), I said to my mother, "I can walk again. Mom, I can work now."

"No, Thanh," she said. "Don't walk until you're better." But we had no money, and even though the pain persisted, I insisted on doing it.

"Mother, I can do it."

She, better than anyone else, knew how poor we had become, so she finally agreed.

The next morning, she made *soi*, and I sold it in front of the house. Since I could not carry the basket, Cong took it for me. But I walked with her, and then she left me by the curb. I sold all of our *soi* that day, and returned with a good bit of money.

After a few more months, I felt well enough to walk to the market and return to my old routine. I would awaken early in the morning, help my mother prepare the food, sell it at the market, and then return with the ingredients for the next day. But we sold no candy at this time. The candy stands that we supplied were too far apart, and I was not yet well enough to walk such distances. Our candy, however, was too profitable to give up, so as soon as I was well enough, I went back to stands, too.

Two years passed, cooking and selling. And then my mother got sick. She caught some kind of flu. But we had no money for a doctor and no money for medicine. For more than a month, mother was very ill. She could no longer work, just lie in bed, so I took over.

Now I awoke even earlier, because my job was to cook the sticky rice. From her bed, she would tell me what to do, and I would bring samples to her so she could see if the rice was ready, or if the banana leaves were the right size. Cong also helped, but I was now 14 years old, so I ran the business.

I worked hard, all morning, all afternoon, and well into the night. I worked everyday, even on Sunday, although I would wait until after church. I no longer had time to go to school, but our relative's wife, Lai, would tutor me in the evenings—one to two hours of instruction, and then another hour or two of homework.

Diep would visit us about once a week or so, and this was a great help. But life was still very hard and our mother was not getting any better, so after a few weeks, Diep decided to move us all back home to Tan Loi. There, mother could go to a good hospital, and my younger brother, sister, and I could be cared for. She said that Tan Loi was now safe for us. The man who had killed our father had been killed in the war.

CHAPTER 7
Apples and Americans

We returned to Tan Loi and moved in with my sister, Diep, and her husband. They had one child and were about to have another, but they could care for all of us. Her husband owned a big rice field, and our other sister, Tien, worked in Saigon and sent us money regularly.

We lived together in Tan Loi for a few months, but then I moved again, this time to Long An, to live with my other sister, Nguon, who needed a babysitter. In Long An, I saw and experienced many things for the first time, but two stand out: apples and Americans.

I remember the Americans very well. I guess I've never quite gotten over them. They were all so tall and so big, nothing like Vietnamese men. Some had blue eyes. And they all seemed to love children. Whenever they saw a child, they would give him or her candy.

They would take one of their big trucks and load it with all kinds of food and candy, park in the center of Long An, hop out, open the back gate, and call to the children, waving their arms and whistling. We'd all run over and wait to see what would happen next.

I remember one time in particular. I was standing at the back of the truck, and a soldier handed me an apple. It was wrapped in purple paper. I opened it. I had never seen anything like it before—such a big piece of fruit, and so red. And the taste—*so* sweet and juicy.

The truck was full of apples, boxes of them, and the soldier wanted to give a box to me. I shook my head "no," but he insisted and showed me by using his arms that he would carry the box for me. He seemed so nice and the apples were so tasty, I agreed. My sister's house was just around the corner, and we walked there together. He carried the box of apples in front of him, talking the entire time. I couldn't understand what he was saying, but I liked him. When we reached the house, he came to the front door with me, put down the box, and left.

I brought it inside and opened it. There must have been 50 apples in the box, each wrapped in purple paper. I gave one to each of my sister's children.

When my sister came home from work, I showed her the apples.

"Where did these come from?" she asked.

"An American," I answered. "I don't know who he is."

I don't think she asked any more questions. The apples were too good, and we had so little. We ate them for weeks.

The American soldiers also gave us many other things we had never seen before—canned bacon, chewing gum, cookies, and powdered milk. They also gave us chocolate and canned spaghetti with tomato sauce, but these we wouldn't eat. They were too different, too strange.

I lived in Long An for about 10 months, until 1969, when I turned 15. It was now time for me to prepare for a profession, and I was going to be a schoolteacher.

CHAPTER 8
Back into the Jungle

My training began in Tan Loi, but after a few weeks, I moved again, this time to My Tho. Here I lived for the next three years, until 1972.

I got my first job when I was 18 years old—teaching first grade at a Catholic school. The school paid me once a month, and I would give all the money to my mother so she could feed and clothe us. She would always give me a little back so I could buy things for myself. I had nice clothes again, and life seemed a little better. I taught at this school for the next two years.

During this time, we lived in a nice new house that my sister Tien had built next door to her house. Tien worked in Saigon, for American Express and also in a bar as a bartender, and she had money to spare. She did this to earn money for the family, but in Vietnam when a girl or young woman worked for an American company, she was considered "no good." People would talk bad about her, and most men would not marry such a girl. But my sister didn't care. The only thing that was important to her was taking care of our mother and our family. Thanks to Tien, mother did not have to work so hard. For this and for so many other reasons, I always loved her.

My First Grade class. I am standing in the center at the back.

Our new house had real walls, not thatched ones. We also had a sofa and a nice bed with a mattress. I did not have to sleep in a bamboo bed anymore, and I was so happy. Once again, we had the best house in our village. That house is still standing today.

We lived there about a year when, one night, the Communists came back. They knocked on the door about 1 a.m. I woke up when I heard them call my mother's name.

Before she answered the door, she came to my bed. She thought I was still asleep, but when she found me awake, she told me to turn my face to the wall and be quiet.

"Pretend that you are asleep," she said, "and that you know nothing." And then she left.

I pulled the blanket over my head and listened. I was so scared. I prayed to God to help us.

Mother went to the door and opened it, and the men walked in and sat down on the sofa. I listened to what they were saying. I could hear very well, because the sofa was just on the other side of the wall next to me. This time, the men had come to collect money. They thought we were rich.

My mother told them that we did not have any money, but they didn't believe her. One man raised his voice, saying,

"If you don't have money," he shouted, "how can you have a new house like this?"

My mother answered that all of her children work very hard and they had built the house for her.

Still, they did not believe her and demanded that she bring money to them in three days. They did not say what would happen if she didn't, but we all knew what their intentions were.

After they left, mother sat in the living room and cried. I cried too, in my bed. I felt so sorry for her—for her hard life with no husband and so many children to care for. When she stopped crying, she came back into the bedroom, and we talked. I told her that I had heard everything, and asked her what we were going to do. She said she didn't know, but she was not scared anymore. We would go into the jungle, even though we didn't have the money they wanted. And we decided that I would go with her.

Just like the last time the two of us had ventured into the jungle, we awoke very early, around 5 a.m. Then we sneaked through the village so that no neighbors or soldiers would see us.

We came to the river, the Tan Loi, and followed the bank to the same spot we'd gone to before, where my sister kept her little wooden boat.

The boat was still there, so we climbed in it. We then pushed away from the shore and mother started to pole us downstream with the drifting leaves, toward the jungle, toward that spot along the river where we had docked before to save my father. We drifted for about 40 minutes—40 minutes of concern over what was going to happen. The last time we had done this, we had gotten away with our lives. But twice?

When we got to that the place on the shore, we got out and walked into the jungle. It was thick and hot and closed in, as before, and we were scared. Eventually, we came to a hut. Two men were waiting for us. They had guns and mean faces. I was so scared. The men talked to my mother and told us to sit down and wait. Somebody else wanted to talk to us. A neighbor of ours was waiting there, too. She had the same problem.

The house that my sister built for our mother

About 10 minutes later, two other men walked over and talked with my mother. They demanded money.

"You have money," one man said to her, "but you're hiding it. Give it to me," he demanded. "The people of our country need it."

"We don't have any money," my mother said. "I'm telling you the truth."

He challenged her. "Where did you get the money for your house?"

"My children gave it to me. They all work."

The man did not believe her.

"Do what you want," she continued. "I do not have any money."

The two men walked away, and we stayed where we were for about an hour. Then the men came back and told us to go deeper to the jungle, farther from the river. Now, fear truly gripped us, but we walked where they told us to go. The jungle was so quiet. We walked for about 20 minutes until we came to a small cluster of houses. There I saw about a dozen people. Families. Men, women, and children, but all Communists. I could tell. And many of the men were crippled. One man had lost his leg. Another had been blinded. And there was one who had no arms. They were soldiers who could no longer fight.

One soldier walked over to us. He looked like the leader. He asked my mother for money, and again, my mother gave the same answer. For some reason, he did not know what to do. I think he believed her, and that's why he did not kill us. He soon let us go, and we walked back through the jungle and returned home as quickly as we could.

Over the next few days, we tried to put this experience behind us, just as we had tried to forget our first trip into the jungle, and all of the other things that had happened to our family over the past three years. But this had been too frightening, and it brought all the sad memories back again.

CHAPTER 9
The Shelling of Tan Loi

The war reached Tan Loi a few months later. A battle broke out between the Communists and soldiers of the old government. Everyone in our village fled to the church. We fled, too. Everyone had the same thought: "There, we'll be safe."

When we arrived, the grounds of the church were already crowded, but the war followed us to this place as well. Our mayor arrived and made an announcement: Everybody had to leave because he had heard that the Communists were going to shell this area in a few hours. In the distance, we could hear the sound of heavy guns.

Crying, we ran, leaving behind everything we had brought. We were so scared. Returning to our house to grab a few things, we continued toward the river, where my brother-in-law kept his boat. When we arrived, the riverbank was full of people. Many of them begged us to take them, but the boat was small and there was only room for our family. No one tried to force their way on. We started the small outboard motor and left, heading toward the city of Cai Mon, we were all relieved, but no one was happy to be forced to escape.

I remember an old man, the grandfather of one of my friends. He was around 70 years old, and was so old and sick, he could not walk. His grandchildren were carrying him, but they soon grew tired and put him down under a mango tree. They asked for help, but nobody could assist them; there were too many people. His daughter was crying. I saw an aunt come over to carry him, but she was unable to move him. They left him there under the tree.

I cried and cried. Nobody knew what I was thinking. I cried because we had to go down the same river as before, toward the jungle, toward the Communists, and I was scared. The shelling was much closer at this time. Earlier in the war, my mother had taught me how to tell if a shell was going to fall nearby or far away. She taught me what to listen for—distant shelling made a "whump" sound and shells that were coming close made a noise like searing meat as they raced toward the ground. The Communists would shell one area, and then move to another site, then continue on. By the time they reached Tan Loi, we were far down the river, but I was still very scared. It took us about an hour to reach Cai Mon.

When we arrived, we stayed in the home of the local priest. He was a good man. When he heard that people could not escape from Tan Loi, he sent boats for them. The boats brought nearly everyone to Cai Mon, but they arrived too late for the old man. He had died under that tree from a heart attack. Again I cried.

The priest's home was very crowded—nearly 100 people had arrived when the fighting started—and most people had to sleep outside. But we were lucky. My mother had found us a spot on the kitchen floor.

There was also not enough food to feed everyone. The first day there, we ate soup and rice, which the priest's family gave to us. But after that, my mother cooked for us, and soon for all the others. She was a good cook and knew how to feed people with whatever was available.

I remember one day when my mother told me and a few other people to pick some water lilies from the river so she could make soup. We filled our arms with the plants and brought them to her. She cooked a big pot of soup for everyone. But I would not eat it.

"Why won't you eat the soup?" she asked.

"This is chicken food," I answered, which was true. Back in Tan Loi, we fed water lilies to the chickens.

"Whatever the birds can eat, people can eat. Haven't I told you this many times? If you're ever lost in the jungle and you get hungry, look for birds and find what they are eating. It will be safe for you.

"Now eat," she continued. "There is a war going on, and we need to do what we can, sleep where we can, and eat what we can to survive. Eat, or you will go hungry."

I took a sip. I did not like it.

"It's not so bad," she told me. "I made it from the tender parts of the plant. Not the tough, outer parts that we feed to chickens."

I ate the rest, and whenever I swallowed, the water lilies made my throat itch. Even today, when I think about this, I can still feel it.

The next day, the church brought over a great deal of food. Enough for everyone. No more water lily soup.

After about three weeks in Cai Mon, we left and went back home. We took a boat back along the Mekong River, and when we arrived at our house, we saw that it had been hit by a shell. The house was, more or less, intact, so we moved back in. But the blast had knocked out many of the nails in the roof—popped them right out of the tin and scattered them on the ground—and when it rained, water came through the holes. And when the wind blew, the roof lifted and bounced above us. Eventually my mother had it fixed. There was also a big hole in my bed from a shell, with shrapnel underneath on the floor. If I had been there during the shelling, I would have been killed. We moved in and tried to live a normal life.

CHAPTER 10
Saigon Falls

On April 30, 1975, Saigon fell to the Communists and everything changed. I'll never forget that day. My mother and I were listening to the radio. I heard people in the streets of Saigon yelling, "We win! We win!"

"Oh, God," my mother wailed. "Oh, God. We will all die."

Two of my sisters lived in Saigon, and my mother feared for their lives. We knew that many people would die that day, and many would flee the country. One sister, Hanh, lived in Saigon with her family, and the other, Tien, worked for American Express. No one knew where they were, or if they were ok. My mother waited for news, but none came. After a few days, she went to Saigon. Hanh was at home and unharmed, but not Tien. Hanh told my mother the news: Tien had fled for America with her American boyfriend. Tien was gone.

The next day, mother returned. I was in church when she reached Tan Loi. I saw her from the window, walking along the road, swerving, shuffling, her head bent down. I ran outside. When I reached her, I almost passed out. She was so heartbroken and sad.

"What happened?" I cried. "What happened?"

"Your sister is gone," she answered. "Hanh is ok, but Tien has left. I don't know where she is." Then she leaned over to me and whispered so that no one else would hear, "She left with her boyfriend, the American."

If anyone else had heard this, there would have been trouble.

And so Tien was now gone. I felt so sorry for my mother. Our father was gone, and now, Tien. We stood in the street and cried.

And then, things got even worse. Because Tien had disappeared, Communist soldiers came to our house and harassed my mother. They would come at all hours of the day and night, banging on the door, yelling, asking questions, and threatening. "Where is she?" they demanded. But we did not know. This went on for months.

Then one day, I was arrested.

CHAPTER 11
Ham Long Prison

When the Communists took over the country, they outlawed all religion. Because I had been a teacher at a Catholic school, one day, three men with guns took me away.

"You need to come with us and take some lessons," the leader said to me. "You need to learn about Communism. About Ho Chi Minh."

They never said that I was going to jail, but I knew what was happening, as did my mother. We begged, pleaded, and cried, but resistance was futile.

"You need to come to our school in a few days, and there you'll be with your colleagues, the nuns from your school, then everything will be alright." The man tried to sound reassuring, but when they left, we were filled with terror. *I was being taken to prison.*

The day soon arrived. My mother had helped me pack a few things that I would need, and we left with two nuns from my school. We walked to an office where a few Communist men filled out some papers. They also told us where to go next.

We walked to Ham Long prison, about five kilometers from Tan Loi. The prison had no gates or locks, but it was still a prison. There was nowhere for me to go if I had fled. The Communists now controlled everything and knew where everyone was and where everyone was supposed to be. If I had left Ham Long, they would have found me and brought me back, and I would have been in bad trouble. I could have run off into the jungle, but there I would have surely died. So I stayed at Ham Long.

Everyone slept on the floor. During the day, we were forced to spend six hours in a classroom so we could learn about Communism. They taught us about Ho Chi Minh, "the wonderful man." Before this experience, I had never even heard of Ho Chi Minh, and now I had to make up for that mistake. I also had to listen to them say terrible things about the Americans—the people who had protected us, fed us, and given us medicine. And I had to listen to lies about the old government and sit there quietly while they insulted the people (like my father) who had worked for them. The Communists tried to indoctrinate me, but I tried not to listen.

To reach this "school," I had to walk a mile each way. We also had to work. The Communists had taken an acre of land in Tan Loi, and we were required to dig it up and turn it into a cemetery for Communist soldiers who had been killed in the war.

The graveyard for Communist soldiers. My son Michael took this picture many years later, not knowing that I had helped to build it.

We worked everyday for many hours, in the rain and the heat, an assembly line of women, digging graves and handing mud from one person to the next. When our workday was over, we would return to our building in Ham Long, but the conditions inside were horrible. The Communists gave us no food; we had to buy our own or have a family member bring some to us. There was never enough to eat. I lived like this for almost three months, until I got too sick to work. I had a high fever and was weak and dizzy. I could barely move. Because of this, they sent me home, but I had to walk. I can't remember how long it took.

CHAPTER 12
Sewing and Love

I was sick for five weeks, but during this time, I decided to learn how to sew. I knew that if I had a useful job, the Communists would not take me away again. There was no tailoring school in my village, so I went to one in the city of My Tho, where I lived with the daughter of a friend of my mother's. An old lady also lived next to us; she was our chaperone. I was now 21, and girls my age could not be left alone in Vietnam.

The school was two miles away. Everyday, I walked there in the morning, walked home for lunch, walked back to school for the afternoon session, and then returned home around 6 p.m. Eight miles, everyday, and since it was summer, it was very hot. This went on for six months. But because I worked hard, learned fast, and did a good job, the teacher hired me to work in her tailor shop for almost two years.

On weekends, I would go home to Tan Loi. One afternoon in 1977, the mailman came and handed me a letter. I looked at it and saw my sister Tien's name in the corner. My heart leaped. She was alive. Then I saw that the return address was somewhere in America.

"Oh my God," I screamed, and ran inside. "Tien is alive! She's alive!"

My sister and brother came over to look, and finally, my mother stood by me. I read the letter to them, and we were all so happy. What a happy day! For the previous two years, we had thought about Tien everyday—wondering where she was, if she were ok, if she were alive. We thought we had lost her, and now, she had been found. Our prayers had been answered.

Life went on, and during the time that I worked in My Tho, I met the man who would become my future husband, Dieu Nguyen. He lived in My Tho, but he also would come to Tan Loi to visit his father, who owned a charter boat. They were a very rich family—as rich as we were poor. They were Buddhist, and we were Catholic, and because of these differences, our families did not like one another. Everyone was opposed to us being together.

But we would get together anyway, although not too often. At that time, there was no social life in Vietnam, and there was very little socialization between men and women. Families did not allow "courting" alone, nor could daughters receive gifts from men. In fact, prior to meeting Dieu, I had never gone out with a man. I had spoken to a few, but that was all. I just was not interested in that sort of thing. I was too busy working.

But Dieu was a good man and very nice, and so we went out on a few dates. Just three or four times, which were considered a lot. We'd go to a restaurant for coffee or dinner. Of course, there was no intimacy, no touching. Sometimes many months went by between our visits. This went on for about three years, from 1975 to 1978.

My mother did not know anything about this, because I knew she would disapprove. Plus, in my country, parents arranged their children's marriages. My sisters had gotten married this way. So one day when I saw Dieu on a bicycle (after not seeing him for almost two years), I told him we should not be together. By that time, his family had arranged a marriage for him, but when he saw the girl, he refused the marriage. Dieu wanted to marry me, so he went to his mother and told her that. Naturally, she was opposed, and she came to my mother to talk to her about this. My mother was also opposed, but there was little they could do to stop us.

Dieu had many arguments with his father over this, but Dieu would not change his mind. Eventually, his father stated that if Dieu and I got married, he would disown him and cut him off from all of the family wealth. His father, and all of Dieu's family, thought that I was only after their money. They would say this to my face on those few occasions when they would even bother speaking to me. But Dieu did not care about the money, and he knew that I did not either, so we became engaged.

Young people in Vietnam have three parties when they are to get married: an engagement party, a second party when people bring gifts, and a third party which is the wedding. Dieu and I had the first two parties, but not the third.

CHAPTER 13
Leaving Vietnam

During this time, the Communists were fighting in Laos. One day, Dieu received a letter telling him that he was to join the army. He hated the Communists and decided that he would not fight for them. This meant death for Dieu, and so, the only thing for him to do was leave Tan Loi. But this, too, was a problem. He would have to move from place to place for the rest of his life, because the Communists would surely hunt him. So Dieu decided to leave Vietnam. Some people were getting out at that time, by boat. He asked me if I wanted to join him.

"No," I answered. "My family needs me. I can't leave them."

"Thanh, you have to go," he responded, and deep down, I knew he was right. Our families were arguing and fighting with us. It was very stressful; I couldn't stand it anymore. There was also no freedom in Vietnam, the Communists had destroyed all that there had been, and had we stayed, Dieu would be captured and killed, or sent to fight.

"Ok. I'll go," I finally agreed. Dieu smiled and said he'd start making the arrangements.

I could not tell my mother or anyone in my family that we were leaving. Word could have leaked out, and that would have been very dangerous for everyone. So I wrote my mother a letter and put it in a clothing bag in my house. I knew that someone would eventually find it after I was gone.

But the night before we were to leave (September 10, 1978), I told my sister, Diep, and her husband of our plans. I told them because they lived next door to mother and could tell her where I'd gone after I had disappeared. I also wanted to hear her promise that she would take care of mother after I had left. We were in the kitchen of her house, preparing vegetables for dinner. This is what I said,

"Diep, Dieu and I are going to leave Vietnam. He can get us on a boat. We want to go to America. I want to be with Tien. She's living there all alone. If we get there safely, I'll send word to you and mom, but we may die. It's very dangerous. So if you hear nothing from us, it means we're dead, and then you need to take care of mom."

Diep was stunned. We both fell into each other's arms and cried. It was so terrible. There was a very good chance we would never see each other again. We cried and prayed together for some time, and she promised to take care of mother. Then we pulled ourselves together and finished preparing the family meal. When we sat down, no one could tell what had happened, or what was about to happen. We were Vietnamese women; we had learned how to pretend and be quiet.

The next day, I went to work at the tailor shop, just like any other day. Dieu had told me that in the morning, a man on a tricycle taxi would come and take me to the boat. He would appear across the street, and I would know him from what he wore—shorts and a hat. When I caught his eye, he would nod at me, and that would be my signal to leave the store and go with him.

The man pulled up across the street a few hours later, peddling a taxi and wearing shorts and a hat. Our eyes met, and he nodded once and then turned away. I turned to grab my things, but just then my sister, Cong, walked into the shop. She never stopped by like that—and today of all days! We talked for a little while, but I was very nervous and it was awkward. The man was waiting for me; I had to leave, yet I could not let my sister know what I was about to do. Soon the tension was more than I could handle, and I started to cry.

"What's wrong?" she asked.

I tried to act like it was nothing serious, but I couldn't hide it, so I blurted out, "Will you take care of mom if I left?"

"Why are you saying that?" she asked. "Are you leaving?"

"I may have to go to another city with Dieu," I answered. "Things between our families are so difficult and unpleasant. I don't think I can take much more."

We were both silent for a moment. She knew very well how things were for Dieu and me.

"So, if I go," I continued, "will you take care of mom?"

"Yes, of course," she answered. Again, we fell silent. I looked outside; the man was still there, but I could see he was impatient.

"Cong, excuse me for just a moment." I walked outside without waiting for her reply. The man looked over at me, and our eyes met. I nodded and with my expression tried to let him know that I was delayed, but was still coming. He nodded back. I knew that he would wait as I walked back inside.

"Cong, I have to get some work done. Can you come back in a few days? We'll have lunch together."

She said she would, and got ready to go.

Before she left, I gave her something. I was wearing a gold cross with a tiny diamond in it. I look it off and handed it to her.

"I want you to have this," I said.

She objected and would not take it, but I insisted. Where I was heading—either to death or America—I would not need it, but she would. She could sell it if things got worse for her in Vietnam.

"I'm tired of it," I claimed, then I put it in a bag and told her again that I wanted her to have it. I was impatient; the man was waiting. I urged her to take it, trying to act as if it were just a little thing of no importance. Finally, she took it from my hand, thanked me, and walked toward the door. We promised to see each other again in a few days.

As she walked out, I looked past her at the man on the tricycle taxi. Our eyes met; again, he nodded. Again, I turned to get my belongings and leave, but just then, my nephew Ngoc ran in the door. He had been sent to come get me because his mother (my sister Hanh) was very sick.

I could not believe what was happening. It was as if God were sending these people to prevent from going away. I didn't know what to do. My sister was sick and needed my help. My mother was old and needed my help. But Dieu was waiting for me, and Tien was in America.

"Please, come," he begged.

It broke my heart, but I had to go and get on that boat. Dieu would be killed if we stayed. But I did have a little money on me, so I gave it to my nephew and told him to take my sister to the hospital, and I would come as soon as I could.

He left, and I ran into the back room, grabbed my belongings, and walked from the store to the man on the taxi. Neither of us spoke. I simply climbed in, and he peddled away.

We moved through the city traffic as quickly as we could. We were late, but we made it to the boat on time. They had waited for me. I think Dieu had something to do with that. When I arrived, he was standing on the roof of the boat, his hands on his hips. He had been looking for me. He was not sure I would come. Probably because I had my own doubts about going. One reason I had come, however, was that he had told me he would come after me if I did not show up.

"I'm not going to relax until I see you get in the boat," he had told me more than once.

The boat was small, too small for the 46 people who were escaping. But Dieu said that this boat would just be used to transfer all of us to a larger boat waiting for us out on the Mekong River, not far from the mouth where it meets the South China Sea. This little boat looked like a typical fishing boat, harmless-looking, but Dieu did not go with me. He would go on the next trip. This way, we would not both be killed if the boat were intercepted by the Communists.

We pulled away from the shore and soon found the other boat. It was not much of a boat. It looked old and worn-out. Its wooden hull was unpainted and patched together, except for the traditional pair of eyes painted on the bow. There was a small section of deck at the stern, a small wooden cabin with a roof, and then an open hold. This is where I sat with the others, while the small boat that had brought us left to get another load of passengers. We waited and tried to get comfortable, but that was not easy. This was a working boat and had no seats for anyone, so we sat wherever we could—on the bottom of the boat (which was wet), on top of our belongings, on a water container, or on a bundle of food.

The night was very dark, which was good—less chance of being caught. But the dark was also frightening. Who knew what was out there? We were all relieved when the little boat returned with more people.

When everyone was in, we expected to go, but there was a problem. We were supposed to meet another boat like ours, also filled with people trying to escape, but it had not yet arrived, and no one knew where it was. We waited, even though we had already been sitting in place for too long. It was very dangerous. We waited for a long time, and for good reason: Six little children were on our boat—all less than seven years old—but their parents were on the other boat. If we left, the children would be orphans. So we waited, listening, looking for the second boat, afraid that we would be caught by the Communists, but the boat never arrived. Around midnight, the captain turned on the engine, and we left.

The children sobbed. We comforted them as best we could, but we never thought of turning back. We had to escape, as did those children.

Later, we found out that the Communists had stopped the second boat earlier that night. They questioned the men in charge, who said they were just fishing. But the Communists told them to turn around and go home, and they did.

CHAPTER 14
Five Days

S lowly we headed down the river, toward the sea. Everyone was quiet—too scared and unhappy to speak. I remember seeing a house that looked very much likes my house. I could see the lights, and I imagined my family back at home. This was very hard, almost more than I could bear. I wanted to go to them, but I could not. Instead, I prayed and asked God to keep them safe. Then we drifted on. The night was very quiet. Suddenly someone on the shore cried out,

"Who's there?"

It was Communist soldiers.

We did not answer. The captain turned off the engine, and everyone got down on the floor of the boat. Then the shooting started. Bullets zipped over our heads. Others slapped the water around us. We drifted on, hoping and praying, until we were out of range and the shooting stopped. Luckily, no one was injured, and the boat was not damaged; and even more important, no one came after us.

Eventually the captain turned the engine back on. We moved steadily down river. After a few hours, we reached the mouth of the Mekong and entered the South China Sea. In a way, this was our final destination. Vietnam was now behind us, and from here, our plan was only to try to reach America, to be free.

I was so naive. I had no idea where America was, or how long it would take us to get there. I thought that I would get in a boat and simply arrive in America. If I thought about anything at all, I thought about my sister, Tien. I had not seen her since she fled Vietnam in 1975. Three long years. In 1977, we received a letter from her, telling us that she was living in America. That was when my dream was born, and I thought only of reaching America and seeing her again. I had her address written on a scrap of paper, hidden in the hem of my blouse, rolled up like a cigarette. If the Communists had found us and learned that I had a sister in America, they would have killed me.

Day One

Out on the ocean, there was nothing to do, nothing to see. So I looked around at the other people on the boat. It was very crowded—46 people on a boat only 11 meters long—but it was hard to tell who anyone was. It was dark. Most people were curled up together with their families. I did know two of them, however. One was the woman for whom I had worked at the tailor shop, and the other was her husband, a former army officer. They were both called Khanh. Dieu had approached them and asked if they wanted to leave. Khanh (the officer) had tried to escape three times before, but had failed each time. Both were eager to get out of Vietnam. *Everyone* on our boat was eager to escape and had paid the owner $1,000 to take them out of Vietnam. Dieu and I, however, had paid nothing because Dieu was a machinist, and they needed him to help run the boat.

The plan was simple: The captain would take us down the Mekong River and out to the South China Sea, and we would travel away from Vietnam until we were picked up by a freighter or, better yet, an American military ship. Our first day on the boat seemed to go ok. We saw one other boat, but they just passed us by. Maybe they saw us. Maybe they didn't.

Day Two

The second day started out much like the first, but that night, a thunderstorm hit the boat. The wind blew hard, the rain beat against us, and high waves rocked us back and forth. We sent the children down toward the bottom of the boat, where we hoped they would be away from the rain and the waves, but everyone else stayed above. We were soaking and miserable. There was just a small roof and little else to keep the rain off. All we could do was huddle together and pray. This brought us together, and I began to notice the other people on the boat. There was such a mix of people. We began to talk a little about who we were and how we had gotten here. Two were former army commanders, who, someone said, had been jailed by the Communists but escaped.

Something else also brought us together: seasickness. Almost everyone was sick, including me, and we cared for each other as best we could. Everyone worried about the children whose parents had been left behind. Children were hit the hardest by the seasickness. One time I got up and checked on them. They all looked dead, but they were just very sick.

Then the engine quit. Dieu quickly crawled below to try and fix it. Everyone was afraid. The images of that night still remain in my mind. The blowing wind, the heavy rain, the waves like walls of water, our battered, leaking boat, the seasickness, the hunger, and the horrible uncertainty about what would happen next. For a long time, we had no idea if we would make it out alive.

Fortunately, Dieu got the engine working, and we began to move again. I was so relieved that I thought the journey would continue without any more problems. But after a while, the captain became so seasick that he could no longer control the boat. Dieu took charge, which meant that he would now need to leave me alone to care for myself. I had gone two days without food or anything to drink. Everyone had brought food and water, but when the storm hit, the water containers fell over, and most of our food spilled out into the oily mess at the bottom of the boat. I did eat some dry noodles that I found floating around, even though they were cold and covered in oil. What little food and water was left, we tried to save for the children. No one knew how long we would be out here. I needed to eat, even though I wasn't hungry. I was throwing up a lot, something yellow from deep inside my stomach came out, and I did not have the strength to move. I thought I was going to die.

After a while, Dieu came down to see how I was feeling. He wanted me to come with him to the deck at the back of the boat, because he felt the air would be good for me. I tried to raise my hand so he could pull me up, but I did not have the strength. I gave up. Dieu had to steer the boat and could not leave his position for very long, so he pulled me to my feet and helped me up onto the deck. I lay there next to him while he steered. The air did help, and after a while, I began to feel better, even though the storm continued to beat on us throughout the night.

Day Three

By the morning of the next day, our third, the storm had not lessened, but at least we were well out into the South China Sea, farther away from Vietnam, and that lifted our spirits. Suddenly our boat hit something big. No one saw what is was, but we all heard it and immediately realized that whatever we had hit had put a hole in the boat. Water was rushing in, quickly ruining our remaining dry food. And the water kept coming. We were sinking. Everyone leaped up and got to work. This was now a life-or-death matter. We used anything we could find to bail the water out—hats, bowls, we even removed our clothes and stuffed them into the hole. But no matter what we did, the water relentlessly kept coming. Such a small hole, yet, in the bottom of the boat, the water was soon above our knees. We all worked feverishly—bailing and passing the water to others on deck—trying to get as much water out as possible. It's amazing how our strength revived so quickly. The fear of death will do that.

We eventually slowed the leak, and I was able to lay back down and rest. I realized—for the first, but not the last time—that even when things were very bad, we would find a way to survive. I began to have hope again.

That night we heard an airplane. Then we saw its lights through the clouds and the rain. Everyone was so happy. We thought that we would be rescued, so we decided to signal them so they would see us and send a boat. But we had no lights and no flares, so we quickly searched to find something to burn. One man and a child still had on dry shirts, so they took them off, and we burned them. But the flames were too small and the smoke too thin; no one on that airplane saw our "SOS."

By now, everyone on the boat had become as close as family. We all experienced the same terror and hopelessness, and shed the same tears. We were no longer the strangers we had been just a few days before.

Our situation was still dire. The storm was still battering us, the boat was still leaking badly, the engine was too wet to run properly, and we were nearly out of food and water. We had seen a few ships, and some had surely seen us, but none had stopped to help us.

Day Four

On the fourth day, we thought we saw a boat coming to rescue us. Our hopes soared, but it turned out to be just a big rock. It was now nighttime and very dark, and we were drifting with no engine. We drifted all night, but in the morning, we realized that we had not gone anywhere. We were still next to that rock. Everyone was so disappointed, but not for long. We still had no engine and were still drifting, and the boat soon collided with the rock. However, the boat held together. The collision somehow pushed us away from the rock. We spent the day drifting on open water. Believe it or not, we were too scared to feel tired or hungry; we just prayed.

Later that day, some of the older people on the boat thought that our prayers had been answered, even though what happened at first filled everyone else with terror.

The storm had ended, and the sea was calm, when suddenly, the water just to our right began to stir. Everyone looked to see what was happening. Just then, an enormous fish rose to the surface no more than five feet from the boat. The size was incredible—longer than our boat and very thick.

"It's a shark," I screamed. "We'll be eaten."

Many of us screamed, and one man ran to get the pistol he'd brought on board.

But Dieu stopped him.

"Don't shoot," he argued. "If you hit it, it could flick its tail and smash the boat."

The man lowered his gun, and just then, an old man spoke up.

"This is no shark," he said in a calm voice. "It's a whale, and it will not harm us."

"Look," he continued, "look to the other side of the boat." We all turned and saw that another giant had risen.

"This is a good sign," he said. "This means that the storm is over, and these whales are here to guide us to safety."

And indeed, it did look that way. Both whales were swimming calmly next to us, heading out to sea. After a while, they disappeared, but the mood on the boat remained high and hopeful.

Rescue

Then arrived the fifth day. When we awoke, Dieu said to me, "Today will be better." The water was calmer, there was just a light rain, and we drifted peacefully. Dieu had predicted right, just by "feeling the air." The years of working on his father's boat had taught him a great deal. The sun soon emerged, and since everyone was soaked, we put our clothes out to dry. I took a clean T-shirt from a woman who remembered that she had one and put it on a pole to collect a little moisture from the sea air. From time to time, we would lower it to the deck, wring out a few drops of water, and moisten our lips. This was all the drinking water we had.

By now people were exhausted, and it showed. We had no water and very little food; no one had any energy. People looked dead, especially the children. The journey also began to take its toll on Dieu. After the captain had become sick, Dieu became our leader, our strength, but now he was beginning to whisper to me that he didn't think he could make it any longer. He had been sitting cross-legged in the same spot for many days, his hands clenched on the wheel. He said that he could not move. There was no longer any feeling in his legs. But he had to continue because no one else could help him with the boat. Everyone who knew anything about piloting the boat was too sick and weak. At one point, a man who was about 50 years old (which is old in my country) and very skinny, offered to steer and give Dieu a rest. Dieu struggled to his feet and made room for the man at the wheel, but the man was too inexperienced and almost capsized the boat. Everyone panicked, so Dieu went back to his place at the wheel.

The good weather was still with us, but everyone was very tired and depressed. We had no hope anymore. We had seen six boats so far, but none of them had stopped to help us. And we were all so hungry and thirsty that some people began to cry that they wanted to go back home. Anything would be better than this. But we couldn't go back. We would all end up in jail, and possibly be killed. Yet, who knew if we would survive out here? The boat was leaking water so badly that if we stopped baling, we'd sink in no time at all.

However, Dieu was strong. He just sat there at the wheel, looking out over the ocean, never saying a word. After a while, the complaining stopped; the boat was quiet.

"I see a boat."

It was Dieu. Everyone stirred and those who could got up and looked. Dieu was pointing at something with his finger.

"There," he said. "The boat is there."

But nobody saw a boat. We thought that maybe he was imagining things. Still, we kept looking and asking, "Where, Dieu? Where is it?"

And then someone else saw it. And then another person, and finally all of us could see it—a large ship. And it was coming toward us. Our spirits soared. Everyone was so happy. We hugged each other and thanked God. This was the seventh ship we had seen over the last few days, but the first to head our way. The other six had raised our hopes—and then dashed them—when they had passed us by. Maybe they had seen us, maybe they had seen that we were just some poor Vietnamese people, maybe we were not worth stopping for. But hope is strong, and we were happy as this ship drew closer. Maybe this ship would stop.

Dieu had been thinking about this and quickly started giving orders. "Bring the children up, and all the men stay down on the bottom of the boat."

People began to move and obey him.

"When they come closer," he explained, "they should see a ship full of women and children. That will make them stop and help us."

The children—about twenty of them—were brought up and placed on the deck and on the roof of the cabin. Most were too weak to lift themselves. Then the men went below, and we waited and watched the ship approach. At one point, we took a blanket and waved to them.

As the boat drew nearer, we could see that the men on deck were white-skinned. They were also looking at us, many of them through binoculars.

"Maybe they're Americans," someone said.

That would be the best. We would then go to America, and I would see my sister, Tien, again.

I was very happy. The boat was coming nearer, and the men were looking at us carefully. They saw nothing but women and children.

The Straat Florida, the Dutch cargo ship that rescued us.

Eventually, they pulled up close to us, about 100 feet away. The ship was huge—long and black with a tall white cabin toward the stern and tall masts for loading and unloading cargo. It was named the *Straat Florida*. From high above, someone on deck spoke to us, but in English, which none of us understood. One man down below, however, did speak some English. He had been a driver for an American soldier during the war. We decided to risk bringing him up, showing that we had men on board.

The man came up and tried to talk to the men on the ship. He listened, and then told us that they wanted to give us food, water, and gas, but they could not pick us up.

We were stunned. Everyone wailed, some fell into each other's arms and many dropped to their knees—some to pray, others to beg. This was more than we could bear. Our boat was sinking, faster than before. We had stopped baling when we thought we were about to be rescued, and now it was too late. Too much water had come in, and everyone on board knew that we were going to sink, and if we sank, we would drown.

I sat down and prayed. I could do nothing else. This was the worst moment of my life since my father had been taken away. I thought this was the end. If they didn't help us, we could go no farther. At one point, I looked up at the ship. I saw the men on deck, and thought that none of them had ever seen anything like this—dozens of people, thin and sick, either begging for help or preparing to die. The sound was terrible— crying, moaning, wailing. I looked up again. Now, more men were on deck looking down at us, including the captain, and many of them were looking at the children—stretched out on the deck, almost naked, thin, and not moving. Many of them looked dead.

By this time, the men on our boat had come up from out of the hold, and some of them were trying to show the men on the ship how many sick children we had on board. They also tried to tell them that our boat was sinking. They begged them to help us.

Finally the sailors understood, as did the captain, who told us to wait while he sent a telegram to his government. By this time, we had figured out that it was a Dutch ship. Not American, but that was ok. Holland would be fine.

We waited and waited, and the men on the ship explained that they had to ask for permission to pick us up. They also encouraged us, told us to be patient, to not give up hope. We waited about half an hour, them looking at us, and us looking at them. Everyone was so nervous. What would the answer be? Would they rescue us, or would they have to leave us to sink and drown?

Our boat was now sinking fast, and the men on the ship could see that. The captain came back, and he could see that, too. Another 10 minutes passed. By now the water in the bottom of the boat was up to my knees. We were going to drown.

Suddenly the captain on the ship gave an order and a wooden ladder and big rope net was lowered down to us. We were told to put the children in there first, and they would lift them up. Then the women, and finally the men. This surprised us. In Vietnam, the men always went first, and women and children last. But we did as we were told, and moved as quickly as we could. They also told us to leave all of our belongings on the boat. Everything. No matter what it was. Some people had brought gold and money, and they had to leave it on the boat. I don't think they minded, however. Everyone just wanted to live.

The Dutch lifted us into their ship as fast as they could

Everyone hurried. Our boat was sinking. The men on our boat helped guide the net and secured the people inside, and the net went up and down—empty and then full, empty and then full again—until everyone was off. Everyone got off in four or five trips. I went up on the third, and Dieu on the fourth or fifth.

The men searched us when we got on deck, and if they found

anything—even a pocketknife—it was taken away. But no one minded. We were alive. Many of us knelt again and thanked God for saving us. We stood on the deck of the big ship for a little while, all together in a group. We were cold, so the men gave us blankets, which we placed on the children.

I remember the last time I saw our boat. I looked over the side. Our boat was drifting away and going down, stern first. I watched it sink, and 10 minutes later—no more—it was gone. They had rescued us just in time.

The boat that took us out of Vietnam, just minutes before it sank.

Suddenly, I felt very tired. And then my legs got weak, and I almost passed out. A man ran over to help me. And then I did pass out and didn't know anything anymore.

CHAPTER 15
Food, Water, Slippers

I woke up in a bed, a real bed with sheets, blankets, and a soft pillow. Opening my eyes, I saw big, white man standing over me. He smiled. There was also a Vietnamese woman there.

"What happened?" I asked her.

"You fainted," she answered.

"This man here is a doctor," she continued, and my eyes filled with tears. At that moment, I knew that I was alive, and that I would live. There would be no more fear and nothing to worry about. I looked around, but didn't see Dieu or anyone else I knew; yet, I felt so happy.

I felt better and walked around the room with the woman. She showed me to the bathroom and told me to bathe. She also said that I should change. The men on the ship had provided some clean clothes for me to wear while they washed my dirty clothes. The shirt was far too large, but again I was happy. I had been wearing the same clothes for five days, and they were filthy and wet and sticky with salt. Until that moment, I had not noticed how uncomfortable I was, but now, I yearned to be clean again.

I took a shower, and it was wonderful, but also very painful. I didn't realize why at first, but then I noticed my hand. It was red and the skin on top was peeling off. Finally, I noticed that my entire body was like this. All my skin was peeling off. The salt water and the sun had done this. I stood under the warm water, and it just fell off in pieces. Later, I found out that I was not the only one with this problem—everyone was suffering. The ship's doctor gave us some cream, which helped.

After I was clean and dressed, I went to find the others. They were in another room. When I walked in, they all smiled at me. The children were sitting up, and they, too, were smiling. Everyone was so happy.

Men from the ship were there, too, and they were all so nice to us. They gave everyone slippers to wear, and they had cooked dinner for us, some kind of soup. Someone said it was supposed to have rice in it, but the doctor had told the cook not to put any in because we hadn't eaten in five days, and the rice could have been too much of a shock to our empty stomachs.

Suddenly I was extremely hungry—something else I hadn't noticed until now—and I devoured the soup right away. It was the best thing I had ever eaten.

An unknown man, my husband Dieu, and myself eating our first hot meal in five days.

Then the children were taken away to let them watch television. They had a color TV on the ship, something the children had never seen. The adults stayed together, and one of the Dutch men explained that they had rescued us without permission from their government. They had done it because they saw that our boat was sinking and knew that we would all drown. For a moment, we were worried. What if permission was denied and they had to send us back to Vietnam? But the man continued and soon said that not long after they had rescued us, they received a telegram from Holland saying that it was ok for them to pick us up.

We were on the boat for 10 days. The ship had cargo to deliver, but the captain decided to change his course and bring us to Singapore, where we would find other Vietnamese refugees and people who could help us.

CHAPTER 16
Singapore

I remember coming into the Singapore harbor. It was so beautiful. Tall buildings and such a blue skies. And the people were working so peacefully. No one seemed worried or afraid.

Before we got out of the boat, we all went to see the captain of our ship. We thanked him for saving our lives. Someone took our picture, and then we said goodbye. Those people are in my heart even today.

On shore, we were met by a group of people who were there to help us. They were tall and blond, maybe Americans, and I think they worked for the Red Cross. We got in a bus, and even though no one knew where we were going, no one was afraid. We could tell that here everything would be ok. The road was new and clean, as was everything else I saw. The buildings were beautiful and looked very solid and strong. I had also never seen so many cars before; hardly any bicycles or motorcycles were evident. Nothing likes the streets in Vietnam. The people seemed so relaxed and happy. Many were just walking around, enjoying themselves. Some people were working at jobs that made the community even more beautiful—cutting the grass, sweeping, and caring for the flowerbeds that lined the road. I also saw people unlike any I had ever seen before. They had very dark skin, but not black like some of the American soldiers I had seen in Vietnam. Their hair was also different, and they wore different clothes. The cloth seemed to wrap around their bodies, and it looked like it did not need any sewing. I wondered how it was put together. On that bus ride, I saw so many new things and had so many questions in my mind.

About an hour later, we arrived at our destination—a camp for Vietnamese refugees. There were thousands of people, which surprised me. I had no idea that so many had gotten out. Many were standing along the road and seemed to be waiting for us. We were very happy to see so many Vietnamese people. We got out of the bus and walked into the camp toward the main building, which looked like an old school building. Our hands were empty. We had nothing, but people came to us and explained what was going to happen.

They would give us $1.00 a day for food, which they said would be enough. The camp officials had a lot of food, and local people would also bring food from their homes, as well as clothes. We would also go fishing in a pond on the property. And we even had ice cream. The ice cream man would come everyday, and this made everyone happy, especially the children.

We did, however, have to find our own pots, bowl, and utensils. We would also need to find our own place to sleep, because the camp was very crowded and there was not enough room available. Families were living together, many in one room. We walked around, looking for some space, and finally found a shed where wood was kept. Nothing fancy, very small, and right next to the toilet, but it was empty, and we were happy.

Dieu and I moved in, along with my former boss, Khanh, and her husband. We cleaned it up and settled in, and once again, I slept on the floor, just like in Kien Hoa with my mother in the chicken shed, and just like in jail. But this was different and much better, except when it rained. The roof was very leaky, so the rain came in. We tried to catch as much water as we could with bowls, but we would all get wet. The toilet would also flood when it rained. The smell was terrible, but what could we do? There was no place else for us to go. So when it rained and things got bad, I would tell myself that I had lived through much worse, and if I could get through this, I would get to America and see my sister again. When I spoke like this to myself, it made me stronger. Plus, there were many people here to help us, to share their food, water, and clothes with us. This was the best part; this made everything bearable. Everyone in the camp helped each other, people who had never known each other before. This was the best.

Sleeping on the floor was no good, though. So Dieu and I would walk around the camp, asking people for empty cardboard boxes which we would lay on the floor to make a bed. Everyone was looking for boxes, however, so they were hard to find, but if you found some and asked for one or two, people would share what they had. I also gathered old cloth, and from this, sewed together a blanket. It was a beautiful blanket. I made it by hand out of hundreds of pieces of cloth—old shirts, rags, and anything else I could find.

These little comforts helped us to feel better, but I was still very sad. I cried so much; all the time, it seems. I lost my appetite and would forget to eat. But Dieu took care of me—cooking and bringing me food, comforting me when I cried. I can see now that I was depressed, but at that time, I just felt homesick. The weather brought on my depression, because it was just like the weather in Vietnam, the weather my mother and brothers and sisters were living in. I thought of them all the time, and I didn't know when I would see them again, or if I ever would. This was very hard. I still had one dream, however—seeing my sister, Tien. This kept me going.

CHAPTER 17
Mail

One day Dieu asked me if I still had my sister's address in America. He thought we should write to her. Maybe she could help by sending us money and helping us get to America.

"Yes," I answered, but then I realized that I did not know where I had put it.

"I don't remember where it is," I told him. "But I gave a copy to you, too. Don't you have it?"

"It's in my wallet," Dieu answered, "but it got wet and ruined. I can't read it anymore."

So it was up to me. *Where had I put it?* For a long time, I could not remember. I was worried and afraid that I would never see my sister again, but finally, I remembered.

"It's in my blouse," I said. "In the hem of my sleeve, rolled up."

I found the blouse and soon found the address. I could still read it; we were so happy. I then wrote my sister a letter, telling her everything that had happened, where we were now, and what it was like here.

The next day we mailed the letter and then began to wait. The first week I knew that it was too soon to expect a reply, but I was still anxious. Everyday I would wake up and wonder if today would be the day I would receive a letter from my sister in America.

After about a week, I started going out to the road to wait for the mailman. We all knew the time when he would arrive, and there would be hundreds of people along both sides of the road, waiting for him. I have never seen people wait for the mailman like that in my life.

We would hear him coming. As he moved along the road toward the camp, people would cheer and yell, "He's coming!" as he came into view. Such pressure, but he was a very friendly man. I guess he knew how excited those people were to see him.

He would walk as close as he could to the camp, and then the people would crowd around him while he called out names. Hands would shoot up and grab at the letters. The person would rip it open, and when the news was good, when they heard from a missing loved one, they would leap and cheer. But when the news was bad, when letters would return as "undeliverable," people would often collapse. I saw people just sit down in the dirt and cry, because they knew that this person, their one hope for life in America or some other great country, would never be found, and they now had nowhere to go.

Dieu and I went to wait for the mail everyday for two weeks—hoping and praying, and always walking away, disappointed. Then suddenly, one day, they called my name.

"Thanh Thi Nguyen!"

I was so happy, I cried. I ran inside with Dieu to get the letter. When I saw my sister's name on the letter, my hand began to shake. And then I saw that the letter had come from America. I was so happy, I cried out.

"It's the letter," I cried. "It's from Tien."

I opened it and read, faster than anything I had ever read in my life.

She told me that her husband had gotten my letter from the mailbox, given it to her, and said, "It's from Singapore" She said she was surprised and confused. She didn't know anyone in Singapore, or so she thought. And then she saw my name—and passed out. Was it true? Was this a dream? For a little while, she didn't know. The last she had heard of me, I lived in a very small town, with no money for a trip to Singapore. How did she get there? In my letter, I explained all of this to her, but my sister kept saying that she read it again and again until she knew that it was true that I was in Singapore.

I could not wait to write her back, so Dieu and I raced back to our place. From then on, Tien and I sent many letters back and forth. She would also send money from time to time, and now life began to get better for us.

I also began to believe that I would see my sister soon, but I would soon learn that that was not to be "soon."

Tien was not an American citizen, and this meant she could not sponsor us. This was a bad blow. I had no idea how hard it was to get to America. I cried. America was my dream. In Vietnam, everyone thought that America was the best and just like heaven. I was so disappointed, but then I looked around and saw many other people who had nowhere at all to go. I felt bad for them, and better for myself. Plus, Tien would work on becoming a U.S. citizen, and then we would go to America. And until that day, we had someplace to go. We soon learned that we could go to the Netherlands, and that the Dutch government would take care of us.

We stayed in Singapore for three months. During that time, Dieu and I got married December 4, 1978. A priest married us in a church, but I had to make my own dress, and we had a very small party.

CHAPTER 18
Holland

About two weeks after we got married, we flew to Holland. Everything was new again. When we arrived there, it was winter, and I learned what that word really meant. Everywhere I looked, I saw white all over the ground and on the road. I didn't know what it was, nor did anyone else I asked. But there was one Dutch lady who had come on the bus to help us. She spoke Vietnamese, having lived there for 18 years. Someone asked her what the white stuff was, and she told us that it was snow. She also explained where it came from, and how it came about.

Next we learned what the word "cold" meant. Before we had left Singapore, the Dutch government had given us some clothes to wear for the winter. They said it was cold in Holland, and all of us would need these clothes. But I grew up in a hot country and didn't know just how cold things could get. So I took only a few things with me. When I arrived in Holland, I quickly learned what a mistake I had made.

They put us all on a bus to go to our new homes. But we drove for a long time, through small towns and far into the woods, and I became scared. I didn't know where we were going; the road was so quiet and there were no people anywhere. I thought they were taking us to jail. I had never seen such emptiness. In Vietnam, there are always people walking around, but here, there was no one.

And then I saw the little houses. They called them bungalows. The woman who spoke Vietnamese told us that this was the place we would live. I was so relieved.

We got out of the bus and waited while they called our name. When our turn came, some Dutch people walked with us to one of the houses. It was small, but it had good walls and a roof, as well as windows and doors; I could see that it would keep us warm. And when they opened the front door and let us in, I saw such wonderful things—a television, soft furniture, a kitchen, a bed, heat, everything. And it was all so nice and clean. They also had food and drinks there for us. I felt so good.

We did have to get used to a few things, such as closing the door. The reason for closing it was obvious—it was cold outside—but this was something new for us. That never happened in my country. We never closed any doors in Vietnam. Only in the evening. We soon adjusted to this and to the many other new things, but life was changing.

I remember the morning when I woke up and looked out my window, and I saw that it was snowing. It was so beautiful that I ran outside in my bare feet to play in it.

We lived in our bungalow for about six months, and then moved to a house in the town of Papendrecht. Here, life got better. My husband, Dieu, found a job, working from 2:00 in the afternoon to 11:00 at night, and I enjoyed having my own place to live. I planted a small garden and would walk around our town to shop in the stores. Our rent was modest, just 350 gelden, which was about $150.

We also started a family. My son was born on September 9, 1979. His name is Michael, and he was the first Vietnamese baby born in Holland. Newspaper reporters came to visit us in the hospital, and the story of his birth was all over the news. And everyday after that, more and more people would come and visit Michael, people we didn't know at all. Many brought gifts, as well as money, but most came just to take a look at him. He was the first Vietnamese baby anyone had ever seen, and they were so impressed by how beautiful he was and how black his hair was.

CHAPTER 19
America

In the summer of 1981, we all went to America to visit my sister. When I got out of the airplane, it was so hot. I could not believe it, since I had gotten used to cooler weather in Holland. We stayed five weeks, and it was wonderful. I fell in love with America right away. I told my sister that this was my dream country. I remember going to an American shopping center. Everything was so big and so full of things to buy. Tien also took me to an American supermarket where I saw so many different kinds of food, and in such great quantities. I could choose any apple I wanted. So different from Holland, and so very different from Vietnam.

"Sponsor me so I can come over," I told her. She said she would, but she would first need to become an American citizen, and that would take some time.

It took five years. My sister became an American citizen, and we arrived in the country on May 30, 1987. Finally, my dream had come true, and I think that there is nothing in the world that can make a person as happy as having a dream come true.

For the first three months, we lived with my sister and her husband in their townhouse in Owings Mills, Maryland. She and her husband, my wonderful brother-in-law, Grant Feusner, helped us with everything we needed.

I remember the first Sunday after we had arrived. My sister told me about all of the jobs that were available in America. Every time my sister drove me up Reisterstown Road, I told her that I liked this road, and that I hoped to someday have my own business here. She said that here in America, you can do whatever you want. If you can't make it here, you can't make it anywhere. You can work two or three jobs, if you want.

Dieu and I got right to work. We started to take English lessons. Dieu got his driver's license just a week after we arrived, and we bought

Grant's old car. Dieu then started looking for a job and soon got one at Maryland Cup, where he worked until 2002.

I also got my driver's license and began working as a tailor at J. Shoenerman, on Reisterstown Road, where I worked for about a year and a half.

One day in April, when the company was closed for the Good Friday holiday, I went shopping at the Valley Center. I saw a dry cleaner there, so I walked in and asked for the owner. A man came out, and we introduced ourselves. His name was Jerry Cohen. I asked him if I could come there to do alterations. I would rent a small space in his store. He then surprised me, telling me that I didn't have to rent.

"You can come here and work," he said, "and we'll split everything you bring in, 50/50."

I was very happy because I now didn't have to worry about paying rent every month. I wanted to take this job, even though my husband and I had just bought a new home on Lantana Drive. We would not have as much money coming in for a while if I took this new job, so I went home to talk to my husband about it. I found him in the backyard, cutting wood.

"Dieu," I said, "I've found a new job and want to quit my old one."

He stopped working and looked up at me.

"What?" he asked. I don't think he could quite believe what he had heard.

"I want to do alterations," I told him, "and eventually open my own business." I then told him my plan. For the first six to twelve months, I did not think I could earn the $150 a week that I was then earning, but I knew that I would be successful soon after that.

"Can I do it?" I asked him.

"Ok," he answered, "if you can earn $50 a week for food, that would be good."

I told him I could and started my business the last week of April. But I didn't make $50 a week. I was only earning $25 a week, month after month. Some days, business was so bad that I made just $5.00. Nobody knew me, but I stayed there in the shop from 10 a.m. to 6 p.m., everyday, six days a week.

I think the owner felt sorry for me, so he would walk around to the clothing stores in the shopping center and ask if anyone needed any alterations, or if they had any customers who did. He did this for me, not for him, and that was very nice. I'll never forget his kindness.

It took me about a year to start making good money. Mr. Cohen then sold his business, and I stayed and worked with the new owner for another six months or so. I then moved to my own shop at 9623 Reisterstown Road, where I work today.

CHAPTER 20
Return to Vietnam

In the summer of 1993, I went back to Vietnam with my sister, Tien, her son Chris, and my son Michael, who was then 13 years old. This would be my first visit back since I had left 16 years earlier, and Michael's first visit and the first time he would see his grandparents. I was so excited about going back, that four months before my departure, I began to have trouble sleeping. I was counting down the days.

It took us 30 hours to fly there, but it did not feel like a long flight. I was too busy thinking about my family, and in particular, about my mother. I wondered what she looked like.

When we landed in Saigon, everything came back to me. I couldn't walk after we landed. I was so scared. I had so many questions in my mind. Would the government arrest me and keep me there? Or would something else happen? I prayed to God, and nothing bad happened. I did notice, though, that everything looked worn-out and poor.

Inside the terminal, we did some paperwork, and then walked out and there, I saw my entire family waiting for us, about 20 people. My sister, Diep, looked old and thin, and my brother was also thin and so dark from working outside. I could tell life was very hard for them. But we didn't speak about any of that, not yet. We just stood there, all holding each other, crying. That moment was unbelievable. I tried to say things to them, but couldn't.

After a little while, we got in a taxi. Now I tried to talk to my sister. I introduced my son to her, and I asked about mother.

"She's at home," she answered, "waiting for us. She couldn't sleep for a month, and for the last three months, she would wake up and everyday go to the calendar and tear off the old day and count the new."

And now the day had come, but first, we had to drive from Saigon to Tan Loi, which took about three hours. When we reached Tan Loi, my heart leaped. I could not wait to see my mother, someone I thought I'd never see again. At one point, my brother told me that my nieces and nephews were waiting for me along the road, about five kilometers from home. They had come by bicycle. When we came to the Tan Loi market, I could see that here things were quite different. Some things I did not recognize at all, and the road seemed smaller because the trees were now so big. The bridge over the river was almost falling down. Finally, we reached our home, and I saw my mother standing in the driveway. She was waiting for us.

We couldn't walk. We couldn't talk. Somehow we met on the driveway, and Tien and I just held our mother and cried. It was so good to see her again. Then mother noticed the two boys, Michael and Chris, her grandsons. She had never seen them before. They walked over to her and both of them gave her a hug.

After a while, Tien and I walked into the house with mother. The rest of my family followed a few yards behind us.

Inside, everything looked exactly the same as before, only now more worn-out and old looking. I walked alone from room to room. It was all the same—the doors, the tables, the chairs, the walls. Nothing had changed. I asked my brother, Danh, "Is everything really the same?"

"Yes," he answered. "When mom heard you were coming, she told us to put everything back where it had been when you lived here. She also had me plant your favorite flowers along the driveway."

I had noticed them earlier. What a special mom ...

That night was the first time in 18 years that our entire family was all together, and it was wonderful. All of my brothers and sisters were there, as well as their spouses and children. About 80 people in all. My mother and sisters and women from our village had been preparing and cooking food for days; we had quite a feast. We also talked and talked for hours, deep into the night. No one could sleep.

This happened almost every night for the next three weeks. After people would get off of work around 5 p.m., they would all gather at mother's house. People would make food (after my sister, Tien, and I had sent someone to buy groceries), and then we would talk. Everyone wanted to know about what had happened to us, and about America. In fact, so many people wanted to ask questions, that they had to take turns. Tien and I would sit at the table, and most everyone else would sit on the floor along the wall. One person would ask a question, we'd answer it, everyone would talk about it for a few moments, and then someone else would ask their question. I soon lost my voice.

Other stories were also told. Old stories, sad stories. Someone asked my mother about how life had been in Kien Hoa during the war—making *soi*, making candy, working all the time, wondering if we would live. She began to talk and tell this story, but the room grew quiet and some people began to cry. Eventually she had to stop, and never did finish. It was too painful.

All of us cried a lot. I cried so much that I became dehydrated and had to be hospitalized for a few days when I came back to Maryland. My mother cried a lot, and I would look in her eyes and think to myself that I could not believe I was home and seeing her again. I also noticed how old she looked. She had been through too much in her life, and it had left its mark on her. I had been though a lot, but it was nothing compared to my mother's suffering.

But I could also see how happy she was. I had been away for 16 years, and my sister Tien for 18 years. During that time, I think she had come to believe that she would never see us again. But now she had her two daughters back, and also two new grandsons.

I remember my sister, Nguon, saying that Jesus had died and come back to life after three days. Tien and I had been dead for 18 years, but now we had come back to life again. I've never forgotten this.

It was a very happy time, but I did have one concern: Michael. He wouldn't eat, never talked, and was very sad. I would ask him, "Michael, what's the matter?," and he would just shake his head. This went on for three days. I was very worried, as was everyone else.

On the third day, around 4 a.m., I found Michael sitting on the floor, crying.

"Michael," I told him, "I think we need to go back to America. You look so sad. You won't eat. You won't say anything. Something is bothering you. What is it? Please, tell me what it is. Please."

Finally, he began to talk.

"Why are they so poor?" he asked. "When my cousins eat dinner, they have only rice. No meat. Nothing else. Why? Why do Chris and I have food and things to drink? Why don't they?"

He had never been to Vietnam and did not know how hard life can be. He now saw what people eat, and how they live. He had seen that his cousins slept on the table. He had seen the pigs and ducks and chickens in the yard and had seen them walk through the house without anyone even noticing. He had seen the Tan Loi River, so muddy and dirty, and had watched people bathe in it and drink from it.

"Michael," I told him, "things are hard here, but your cousins are alright. I work hard at home and send them money so they don't have to suffer. Don't worry, they'll be fine."

This made him feel better. It also helped me, and helps me even today to focus on what I need to do. Life is still very hard for my mother, my brothers and sisters, and their children, but I do believe that they will be fine. The war is over. They also work very hard and can take care of themselves. And I do as much as I can for them, just like I always have. I don't make *soi* any more, or sell candy to the street vendors, but I work hard in America and send them money so they can buy what they need.

We talk on the phone, and I feel so close to them. I also come back to Vietnam to visit, every two years or so. And, of course, I think of them everyday, and remember the life we've lived together, our struggles, our tragedies, and our survival.

My Mom

These are pictures that I took when I returned to Viet Nam again in 1998. While there, I visited the center and talked with many of the

staff and the patients. The legend accompanying each picture gives more details.

I have been sending money regularly to help support this Leprosy Center since 1998.

Part of the proceeds from the sale of this book will be used to continue this support.

This is my last dream.

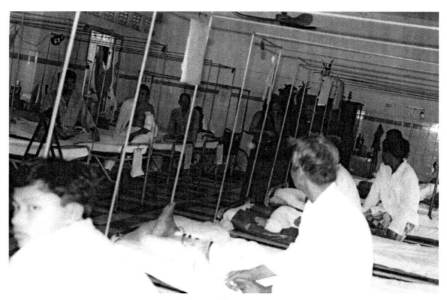

My first visit to the Leprosy Center

This patient has lost her sight and one arm from Leprosy

This patient is showing me how she can sew.

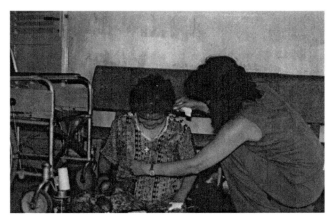

I gave her gift of a Rosary after she showed me how she could still although she has lost both her hands and her legs.

The Priest who has spent his whole career running the Leprosy Center along with 12 Nuns

3358963